Christian Ministry
and the
Fifth Step

About the author:

Ed Sellner received his doctorate in Pastoral Theology from the University of Notre Dame in 1981. He first became interested in that field and in Fifth Step ministry in particular while involved in a year of clinical pastoral education at Willmar State Hospital and Hazelden. Since then he has counseled recovering chemically dependent people and their families in Indiana and Minnesota, and helped plan and implement training workshops for the Hazelden Continuing Education Department. He has also taught pastoral theology courses at Notre Dame and St. Catherine's College in St. Paul and written for various pastoral publications.

About the booklet:

"As more and more chemically dependent people and their family members ask ministers to listen to their Fifth Steps, it is important that ministers receive some guidance. This booklet is written with the hope of providing some insight into this important area of pastoral care. The general principles outlined here, however, really apply to anyone who seeks to be of help as a listener in the event of self-revelation called the Fifth Step . . ."
—from the author's Introduction

Professional Education

Christian Ministry and the Fifth Step

by
Dr. Edward C. Sellner

First published, June, 1981.

ISBN: 0-89486-130-1

Printed in the United States of America.

Table of Contents

Introduction

Whether one chooses to call alcoholism a progressive illness, an addiction, a disease or an allergy, it is one of society's greatest public health problems, affecting millions of lives each year. Although the price society pays can be measured in financial terms, the cost in human suffering is extremely high. In America in 1935, however, the phenomenon of alcoholism, which transcends the boundaries of race, class, intelligence, and creed, found a worthy antagonist in Alcoholics Anonymous. A movement profoundly American in its pragmatism and pluralism, Alcoholics Anonymous (A.A.) offers a way out for those suffering from the tragic effects of alcoholism.*

As a pastoral theologian whose ideas of Christian ministry have been greatly influenced by my work with recovering A.A. and Al-Anon people, I have studied the early history of A.A. and discussed its recovery process with former Hazelden patients as well as other Christian ministers. What has become clear in my dialogue with history and contemporary experience is how closely A.A. and Christianity are related, and how much they have learned and can continue to learn from each other.

*See *Not-God: A History of Alcoholics Anonymous* by Ernest Kurtz, available from Hazelden Educational Services, for a full treatment of the development of A.A.

Without denying the genius of A.A.'s co-founders, William Griffith Wilson (Bill W.) and Robert Holbrook Smith (Dr. Bob), the early word-of-mouth program which they used to help rehabilitate alcoholics like themselves was largely based upon Christian principles articulated by the Oxford Group Movement, a Christian evangelical movement which emphasized surrender and confession as prerequisites of positive change.[1] There was also the profound influence certain Christian men and women had upon the personal lives of A.A.'s founders themselves—from the Episcopalian priest, Sam Shoemaker, to the Roman Catholic nun, Sister Ignatia, to the Jesuit priest, Father Ed Dowling. Though Bill Wilson, according to his own words, "always carried a certain amount of prejudice against churches and clergymen and their concept of God," he acknowledges in his history of A.A. that "without clergymen A.A. could never have started in the first place."[2]

Evidently, the learning process was and is reciprocal. As many chaplains, pastors, clergy trainees and lay ministers admit, they have gained tremendous insight into their own Christian heritage and concept of ministry through their contact with A.A.'s Twelve Steps and the friendship of recovering people. Many of them, perhaps for the first time, have discovered and learned to accept their own limitations, powerlessness and creaturehood. Many have experienced a new personal freedom when they surrendered their lives as Step Three suggests, and the healing power and presence of God when they first participated in Step Five. Ultimately, many have experienced a transformation in their image of God, from a Higher Power once felt as threatening, punitive, and judgmental, to One who is loving, welcoming and forgiving. Thus, while A.A. has learned from Christianity, so have Christian ministers learned from A.A. The underlying presupposition of this booklet is that this learning, based on mutual respect, dialogue, and the sharing of experiences, needs to continue for the benefit of both the fellowship and the church.

More specifically, this booklet is written for Christian ministers who want to know more about A.A.'s Fifth Step and the ministry of reconciliation associated with it; what they can do to become more effective ministers and signs of reconciliation in people's lives. As more and more chemically dependent people and their family members ask ministers to listen to their Fifth Steps, it is important that ministers receive some guidance. This booklet is written with the hope of providing some insight into this important area of pastoral care for those whose Higher Power has already been identified with a loving father, a human face, a holy spirit. The general principles outlined here, however, really apply to anyone who seeks to be of help as a listener in the event of self-revelation called the Fifth Step—no matter what their religious beliefs or understanding of that Higher Power.

The Fifth Step: Telling All of One's Story

Alcoholics Anonymous began when two people revealed themselves to each other and shared their life stories. As one of the founders later wrote, "The spark that was to flare into the first A.A. group was struck at Akron, Ohio, in June 1935, during a talk between a New York stockbroker and an Akron physician."[3]

From that simple event of sharing, A.A. grew into a fellowship of over thirty thousand groups worldwide and over a million members. In sharing stories A.A. found its definition and purpose: "Alcoholics Anonymous is a fellowship of men and women who share their experience, strength, and hope with each other that they may solve their common problems and help others to recover from alcoholism."[4]

This method of helping others *and oneself* through sharing experiences is an important, if not essential, part of A.A.'s ongoing existence. It is the way members of A.A. minister to each other and help to guarantee their ongoing recovery. It is in this context of story-telling that the Fifth Step must be considered and, as we shall see, the ministry of reconciliation associated with it.*

In order to better understand what the Fifth Step is about, let us begin with a brief examination of pertinent A.A. literature which describes the Fifth Step: "Admitted to God, to ourselves, and to another human being the exact nature of our wrongs." Although a summary is given here, anyone who plans on Fifth Step ministry should read A.A.'s two primary sources, *Alcoholics Anonymous* (affectionately referred to by A.A. members as "the Big Book") and *Twelve Steps and Twelve Traditions*, both written by Bill Wilson. They contain the most complete "official" explanation of Step Five.[5]

---

*The opinions expressed are solely those of the author and do not represent A.A. as a whole.

Both sources reveal that the Fifth Step is but one Step leading to "spiritual awakening," a term defined as a personality change or transformation, a new state of consciousness and being, a profound alteration in one's reaction to life. In short, it is what Bill Wilson himself called "a mysterious process of conversion, . . . the very thing most alcoholics have sworn they never would have."⁶ However spiritual awakening is defined (and there may be as many definitions as there are people who have had them), the Fifth Step, though only one Step, is one of the most necessary to long-term sobriety and peace of mind. It is considered "vital," since without it the chemically dependent person may never overcome the compulsion to drink. Unless a person tells *all* his* life story, the Big Book says, invariably he gets drunk again. What, then, are some of those things which should be acknowledged in Step Five?

The Fifth Step is concerned with the admission of all those areas of a person's life which arose in Step Four's "searching and fearless moral inventory." Though the Fifth Step's wording states that only "wrongs" be admitted, the explanation of it offered by Bill Wilson obviously goes beyond strictly moral categories. What is to be admitted includes: (1) memories: "every dark cranny of the past," all those "tormenting ghosts of yesterday"; (2) character defects: every twist, obstacle, weak item, defect that has come to light during Step Four; (3) feelings of guilt: "the open and honest sharing" of its "terrible burden"; (4) all those things which "really bother" a person, since if one attempts to carry the burden alone the very concealment leads to increased anxiety, remorse, depression, tension, and irritability. (Here the Fifth Step listener should be especially aware of loss in a person's life and the need to acknowledge the feelings often associated with it, such as grief, anger and resentments which perhaps remain unreconciled.) Another important part of Step Five,

*To avoid the cumbersome "he/she" pronoun, the alcoholic and the Christian minister are generally referred to in the male gender throughout the text.

although A.A. writings don't specifically mention it in regard to this Step, is the acknowledgement of personal assets and attributes in addition to obstacles and character defects. In that way, the *entire* story is told, since everyone has God-given talents and strengths which need to be claimed, accepted and affirmed. Without this attempt at balancing assets with defects, Step Five itself becomes distorted; confirming the negative feelings and low self-esteem which most chemically dependent people already have when they begin their Fifth Step.

What can happen when a person's story is shared with another? A.A. lists a number of possible results: (1) an end to the compulsion to drink or abuse drugs; (2) increased self-knowledge based on honesty and realism; (3) new self-confidence; (4) relief and release from feelings of guilt; (5) delight; (6) humility; (7) loss of fear; (8) an experience of healing tranquility; (9) the ability to begin to forgive others and oneself; (10) a sense of gratitude; (11) emergence from a terrible sense of isolation; (12) the beginning of a new God-consciousness, sometimes for the first time:

> Many an A.A., once agnostic or atheist, tells us that it was during this stage of Step Five that he first actually felt the presence of God. And even those who had faith already often became conscious of God as they never were before.[7]

Considering these results, we can see the telling of all of one's story with the help of another person can be, at least theoretically, a very significant event of reconciliation. It is also evidently an event which is not meant to occur only once in a recovering person's life, since Bill Wilson's explanation of Step Ten reminds us that annual and/or semiannual "housecleanings" are worthwhile.[8] They help the recovery process, the conversion-reconciliation process, continue.

Now that we have gained some understanding of what constitutes Step Five, let us turn to a consideration of the ministry which can be associated with it. As I see it, such Fifth Step ministry can be described in its entirety as a process involving three movements. The first, "becoming a friend," is when the minister makes himself available to accept another person's life story; the second movement, "discerning and guiding," is when the minister listens to the story offered and holds it gently for awhile; the third, concerned with Step Five's conclusion, is when the minister as a living sign of reconciliation affirms that story and returns it to the teller—with the understanding that only he or she can live it out humbly and gratefully. Although all three movements necessarily overlap and are meant to be integrated in the personality of the minister, let us examine each movement separately.

Ministry Before Step Five: Becoming a Friend

A.A. literature states that almost anyone can serve as a Fifth Step listener or minister: an A.A. sponsor, a clergyperson, a doctor, a psychologist, a family member, a friend—even a stranger will do for some. Whoever is chosen, however, should have certain qualities which are considered necessary for such a task. These qualities include: (1) an ability to keep things in confidence, to be "closemouthed"; (2) an understanding that Step Five is a potentially significant event for any recovering person; (3) some degree of wisdom and maturity based upon previous constructive handling of chemical dependency and/or other serious problems in the listener's own life; (4) a willingness to share himself and his story with the one who is taking Step Five. (This latter sharing has certain advantages, as A.A. literature subtly suggests in its advice to the one who is about to participate in the Fifth: "Your listener may well tell a story or two about himself which will place you even more at ease.")[9]

Putting together all these qualities advocated by A.A. for the Fifth Step listener, the model of ministry which emerges is that of becoming a friend and developing a relationship of friendship with those whom one is to serve in Step Five. As A.A. writings suggest to anyone who wants to be of help, "never talk down to an alcoholic from any moral or spiritual hilltop"; rather, "offer him friendship and fellowship."[10] The wisdom of this model of ministry is confirmed by the ongoing experiences of A.A. and Al-Anon members, as well as by more formal research studies.[11] If people are to come to the Christian minister for Fifth Steps, the minister must already be perceived as a friend: someone whom others feel that they can turn to, confide in, share without fear of condemnation those often painful, disruptive dimensions of their lives.

This means that ministers must be available and willing to share themselves, not only in liturgical events, sermons, and homilies (as important as these can be), but also in words and deeds outside of sacraments and liturgies. This does not necessarily mean that the minister must be close friends with many people since that is an impossibility; nor does it mean that his "story" constantly and egotistically dominates every conversation. Rather, he should be someone with whom others feel welcome, and like themselves, in search of holiness and God; someone in the ancient tradition of the soul-friend who is a "spiritual teacher," or someone like Henri Nouwen's "wounded healer" who offers himself as a spiritual guide.[12] Only if a person is already to some degree a friend and guide will he elicit a response of openness when people seek to participate in Step Five, to discern and express the estrangement in their lives. If they perceive their Christian ministers as aloof, distant, paternalistic, or condescending people, they will not seek them out for Fifth Step listeners— nd matter how much the minister may know intellectually about A.A. and its recovery process.

Thus, if you hope to become an effective Fifth Step guide, you must first take the time to get to know the people associated with A.A. and Al-Anon, and those in your congregation who are having trouble with chemical dependency. If you are acting as a chaplain in a residential or outpatient program, you should also make the effort to get acquainted with the Fifth Step participants *before* the Fifth Step—if at all possible. That effort alone can make the difference between a positive Fifth Step leading to an experience of reconciliation encompassing mind and heart, or one predominantly characterized by anxiety, defensiveness, and the inability of the participant to reveal all that needs to be 'told. Familiarity and friendship foster openness, trust and greater self-disclosure; much depends upon whether the Fifth Step participants perceive you as a friend or stranger to them. The prodigal son's story shows that the courage to take a step of self-revelation, to make a journey home, to reveal oneself to another in the hope of being welcomed back depends to a great degree upon a previous relationship of some familiarity and trust. It depends upon whether the minister has *already* manifested in his life those important qualities associated with a friendship before the event takes place.

One quality in particular which can and should be associated with a ministry of friendship is that of acceptance, or what the Swiss psychiatrist, Carl Jung, calls "unprejudiced objectivity." He defines the term in his writings as not a purely intellectual, abstract attitude of the mind, but as a "kind of respect for the facts, for the man who suffers from them, and for the riddle of such a man's life." "The truly religious person has this attitude," Jung tells us in *Psychology and Religion: West and East.* "He knows that God has brought all sorts of strange and inconceivable things to pass and seeks in the most curious way to enter a man's heart." Thus, if you want to guide another in any kind of self-revelatory event (surely, this would apply to A.A.'s Fifth Step), according to Jung you must first accept the other person, even the very worst aspects of him:

> If the doctor wants to guide another, or even accompany him a step of the way, he must *feel* with that person's psyche. He never feels it when he passes judgment. Whether he puts his judgments into words or keeps them to himself makes not the slightest difference . . .
> We cannot change anything unless we accept it. Condemnation does not liberate, it oppresses. I am the oppressor of the person I condemn, not his friend and fellow-sufferer.[13]

Jung makes it clear that he is not saying one must never make judgments or confrontations, but that they should only be made in the context of an accepting relationship *first*; that is, a relationship of mutual respect and trust, of friendship.

Jung also stresses that such acceptance of and friendship with others begins with oneself: "Be the man through whom you wish to influence others."[14] Paraphrased for the Fifth Step minister: "If you wish to influence others as a friend, you must first befriend yourself." For Fifth Step ministers, this means taking the time to discern your own weaknesses and strengths, attempting to gain a knowledge of and familiarity with your own personality and heart, learning to appreciate the tapestry which makes up your own life story: the significant events and persons, the good times and bad, the turning points. This process of discernment can be accomplished by writing out your own Fourth Step (if you have not done so already) and sharing all of your story with another minister/friend in a Fifth Step event. Other exercises in reflection and self-awareness[15] can also be done as your story continues to unfold. These suggestions presuppose that only in recognizing and accepting your own "wounds" will you be able to recognize and help others who are also wounded and struggling. Only if you have already seen and to some degree accepted yourself will you be able to manifest the quality of acceptance and friendship advocated by Jung and A.A.

This model of ministry, this vocation of befriending those in need, is as old as the Church itself. It is rooted in the words of Jesus. "I call you friends," he told his group of followers. "Love one another as I have loved you" (John 15: 12-17). It is a vocation echoed in the words of St. Paul:

> Be friends with one another, and kind, forgiving each other as readily as God forgave you in Christ. Try then to imitate God, as children of his that he loves, and follow Christ by loving as He loved you (Ephesians 4: 32-6: 1-2).

A vocation which all Christians share, and one which developed through the centuries into a specific ministry of spiritual discernment or soul friendship, it is this calling which is so closely related to the ministry of the Fifth Step. By reflecting on that ancient tradition as well as their own life stories, Fifth Step ministers ultimately learn the meaning of compassion and care and are transformed from people with unrealistic expectations of curing others to people who have learned to wait patiently for the healing power of God. Associated with the quality of acceptance, it is those qualities of care, compassion, and especially patience which form the basis of all ministry. It is with them that Fifth Step ministry begins.

Ministry During the Fifth Step: Discerning and Guiding the Story

If Step Five is an opportunity for the recovering person to tell his life story, to acknowledge all those things which need to be recognized and accepted before they can be reconciled, then ministry in the Fifth Step can be seen as primarily that of facilitating the story-telling process. One of the biggest blocks to such self-disclosure and such ministry, however, is the presence of fear: the fear of being known in all one's human frailty and failures, an experience of spiritual nakedness which can be much more threatening than merely being without clothes. When you begin to get involved in Fifth Step ministry, you need to be aware of the power of this fear, and how interrelated it is with the recovering person's own poor self-image. You also need to be aware of how difficult it is for the recovering alcoholic or chemically dependent person to acknowledge in Step Four any attributes and assets he might have—in addition to those liabilities and defects. That very exercise is often merely an intellectual one, since the genuine experience of claiming those gifts, strengths and reasons to be grateful, often only follows the Fifth Step itself. Thus, many begin their Step Five feeling very guilty, remorseful, ashamed and—because the minister may represent for them all the "shoulds" and "should nots" of their formation—extremely cautious and afraid. Since the ultimate purpose of Step Five is to help another experience some degree of reconciliation, it is your responsibility as the minister/listener to help that process of self-disclosure along in whatever way you can. The following suggestions may contribute to this revelatory process.

The first thing to be considered in the Fifth Step ministry is the place where the event will occur. As a responsible guide, you need to find a room that fosters dialogue, has a warm atmosphere (perhaps your office or study), certainly one that is comfortable and softly lighted. You also need to arrange the chairs in such a way that participants are facing each other, since the encounter itself is meant to be a dialectical process in which both people are involved. No desk or other physical barrier should stand directly between the two of you. Once this attention to the location and setting of the Fifth Step is taken care of, the event of self-revelation can begin.

Even if you have already made an effort at getting acquainted with the Fifth Step participant, it is still necessary to have some form of introduction in order to make the person feel welcome and more at ease. This can be done most effectively with words of greeting as well as a warm handshake, both of which combine to show that you are looking forward to this time together rather than resenting it as an imposition. Once the two of you are seated, you should cover various topics so that the other knows what to expect from you and what you expect of him. In whatever order these topics are put, you should allow for the spontaneity of the encounter and at the same time realize that this initial phase is meant to be brief. (If you have met previously with the participant in a Fourth Step preparation session, much of what is suggested here, of course, would already have been covered.) Thus, before the participant begins to tell his story, such topics as the following should be discussed:

1. Your previous experience: a statement about how you got involved in Fifth Step ministry, the possible personal meaning you find in A.A.'s Twelve Steps, and/or the respect you have for people attempting to become reconciled with their lives. This should not be done in a patronizing way, but merely as an honest attempt to establish some rapport.

2. The participant's feelings: already aware of the anxiety people have when taking their Fifth Step (often for the first time), you should make some effort of asking how the other person is feeling about Step Five, and allow him to freely express any hesitations, questions, fears.

3. The role of the minister: you need to tell the participant that your role is primarily one of listening to and discerning the other's story. To facilitate this process, you might interrupt at times if something is unclear or if you think the participant should describe in more depth some relationship or event that could be significant. Also, since you will be making an attempt at the conclusion of Step Five to briefly summarize the story you have heard and perhaps help the other discern any patterns of estrangement or positive attributes, you will be taking some notes during the encounter—notes, however, which will be given to the participant at the end. Above all, you do not see yourself as a judge, someone passing judgment on the character and life of the individual, but rather as someone who wants to accept and help him in whatever way you can. Also, what is revealed in Step Five will remain confidential—something shared only between the two of you and God.

4. Your expectations of the participant: you should present your expectations of the other as briefly as possible, preferably in a few short sentences rather than in a way which overwhelms. These "suggestions" you offer, however, are meant to guarantee that the participant does have a good Fifth Step. Thus, you should state that you (1) expect the participant to be as honest as possible; (2) that the participant acknowledge *all* those things which stand in the way of his feeling good about himself, especially the areas of his life and personality that he might prefer to keep concealed; (3)

that he should be specific and concrete in his examples of such things as resentments, fears, pride; (4) that towards the end of the Fifth Step, he should discuss what positive things are at work in his life, what strengths and talents he has to offer others, what reasons he might have to give thanks.

5. Length of Step Five: because the Fifth Step is potentially a very therapeutic event, you should state that as much time as is necessary will be given for this important Step. If time, however, is definitely limited, you should clearly state how much is available—with the assurance that another session can be set up. Fifth Steps vary; sometimes a person can say what needs to be said in half an hour, more commonly in an hour and a half; sometimes two or three hours. Beyond that is a sign that the person does not have a clear idea of what can and should be covered in Step Five, that he has not taken the time to set priorities, or that he may be overscrupulous and seeking the approval of the listener rather than attempting to clearly define the unreconciled areas of his life. It can also mean that the minister himself is being *too much* of a non-directive guide.

6. Encouragement: some words of encouragement should be given before the participant actually begins his story. You can advise him to relax and let the story flow, perhaps suggesting if this is his first Fifth Step that the participant start with his early childhood: when and where he was born, how many are in his family, and what sort of memories he has of those early years. This not only makes it easier for the other to get into the story-telling, but easier too for the listener to understand the participant, and gain a broader picture of his life.

Once the participant has begun his Fifth Step, you begin your own process of discernment as you listen attentively to the story that unfolds. In the ancient tradition of the *anmchara*, the soul friend, you seek to discern the person's heart and the life journey that person is on. Listening closely to what is being said, ask yourself a number of crucial questions: (1) is this person willing to change and in the process of doing so? (2) does he see himself in a realistic way or is he still blinded with self-delusions? (3) is he truly coming to accept himself as he is with both good and bad qualities, weaknesses and strengths, defects and assets? (4) is his journey beginning to be characterized more by trust than fear, hope than despair, community than isolation; more by forgiveness of others than by resentments against them?

Like a physician, you also seek to discover any patterns of alienation which emerge as the story is told: any recurring themes of anger, resentment or fear that might provide insight into a self-destructive way of living, or any inner wounds which still need to be recognized and healed. Aware that strengths and weaknesses are so closely intertwined, you also seek to discern the talents and assets sometimes hidden within the fabric of a person's life which need to be acknowledged and affirmed. You seek, in effect, to make *connections* with perhaps isolated events, examples, and characteristics as they're told. While you're listening, take notes for greater recall, interrupt when something is unclear, sometimes challenge in a non-threatening manner if the person is not being specific or concrete. Above all, allow the other the space to tell his story as you accept without embarrassment whatever is acknowledged, allowing the free expression of feelings and of tears.

Besides listening and discerning, the ministry involved during the Fifth Step includes the sharing of your story when and where appropriate. This sharing not only puts the other person more at ease (as previously mentioned), but also gives him the distinct impression that he is *not alone* in this event

nor on his journey toward wholeness, holiness, and God.
As Jung says about anyone participating in healing therapy,
the effective helper needs to "emerge from his anonymity
and give an account of himself," in no way acting as "the
superior wise man, judge, and counselor." "It makes all the
difference," according to him, whether the healing helper
"sees himself as part of the drama, or cloaks himself in his
authority."[16] It is precisely your willingness to share examples
from your own story that creates a relationship of trust, a
sense of common-union, of friendship between participants.
Such a relationship fosters dialogue which makes full
self-disclosure a greater possibility—only when there is no
fear of condemnation can people identify and fully
acknowledge the painful reality of their pasts. Such sharing
ultimately can result in reconciliation—not just a theoretical
concept, but an experience of healing and forgiveness. That
experience, according to the theologian, Paul Tillich, is the
greatest one anyone can have; it is "the fundamental
experience in any encounter with God."[17]

Concluding Step Five: The Ministry of Being a Sign

As the Fifth Step draws to a close, the last movement of
"returning the story to the giver" includes three phases: (1)
helping the other discern the positive in his life; (2)
summarizing what the minister has heard; and, finally, (3)
giving him some form of sign that he is still accepted despite
anything he's felt, said, or done. All of these latter phases
make up a totality: the ministry of being a sign of
reconciliation for those participating in Step Five. Let us
briefly consider each phase as named.

Phase I: When you perceive that the Fifth Step participant has nearly completed the telling of his story, it is your task to make the transition from the focus on the past to a discussion of the present and future. First ask the participant to concentrate on the positive characteristics which he has going for him as well as any reasons he might have for being grateful. This is a mutual discernment process. If necessary, point out various assets and attributes you saw emerging from his story. As already mentioned, the person finishing Step Five may have overlooked this positive aspect in his previous Fourth Step preparation or, with feelings of guilt and remorse, may not be aware of any positive traits. If you have been listening closely throughout Step Five, you should be able to offer some encouragement and suggestions—never, however, resorting to "sugar-coating" the reality of a person's life nor placing unduly optimistic interpretations on what you have heard. When helping another person discern and affirm the total picture, loving realism is the best gift you can offer.

Once this discussion of the positive has taken place, you ask about the other's future plans: what sort of ongoing recovery program has he designed for himself? Here you should help the participant be specific, especially directing him toward participation in A.A. and/or Al-Anon groups. You also should make it clear that Step Five, no matter how worthwhile, is not a panacea for the recovering person; if he wants to continue sobriety and personal growth, he must realize the need for others in his life and the rest of the Twelve Steps. State this clearly and firmly as a friend who cares about the other's future.

Phase II: After sufficient time has been spent in this positive and realistic discernment (time, of course, which varies according to the individual's needs and your intuition of them), briefly summarize what you have heard as the story unfolded. This form of feedback is an essential part of the entire discernment process which you have been involved in since the beginning of Step Five. It is your opportunity to share with the other person what you think he should be aware of but has perhaps overlooked; what struck you as significant; what patterns of behavior, feelings, attitudes emerged which might help the participant get a better understanding of himself. This form of "returning the story" should always be done provisionally and tentatively, making it clear that you do not pretend to hold the key to another's life; that no matter how well-trained anyone is, he cannot fully grasp what has happened nor what should happen for another person. That mystery rests with each individual and his Higher Power. While sharing what you have perceived, however, you seek some response from the participant in terms of agreement or disagreement, so that *together* you might discover some important insights which "click" or make sense.

Above all, this feedback phase is not meant to be a time of condemnation, but an opportunity for showing that you have heard carefully and compassionately what the other has shared, that you respect that story and accept it in its entirety without covering up or minimizing what has been acknowledged. This is especially true in regard to feelings of guilt. "Being accepted," according to Tillich, "does not mean that guilt is denied." In his book, *The Courage To Be,* he wisely says:

> The healing helper who tried to convince his patient that he was really not guilty would do him a great disservice. He would prevent him from taking his guilt into his self-affirmation. He may help him to transform displaced, neurotic guilt feelings into genuine ones which are, so

to speak, put in the right place, but he cannot tell him that there is no guilt in him. He accepts the patient into his communion without condemning anything and without covering up anything.[18]

Phase III: In this stage you return to that quality so important to the minister and the ministry of Step Five: the human quality of acceptance advocated by psychologists and theologians alike. Essential to the Fifth Step before and during the encounter, this acceptance must be *externally* manifest, put into audible words and visible signs, especially at the Fifth Step's conclusion. Inasmuch as any of us needs to say things, to speak things out before we can be freed of them, we also need to hear and see that despite all our human frailties and failures we are still accepted, forgiven and loved. This psychological insight is affirmed by the wisdom of early church communities which acknowledged the importance of their members' rehabilitation process culminating with words of forgiveness and some form of visible sign.[19] Aware of this, you can reaffirm the power of the word and the value of the sign in this event. Often, in fact, unless some positive words are given and some form of sign made, people won't truly *experience* reconciliation.

Thus, after everything else has been said, after both the liabilities and assets have been discerned and the story told, you should end the Fifth Step with some accepting words, such as, "Whatever you've done, it's behind you; what's past is past, it's time to look ahead; God accepts you and loves you despite everything." Along with the words can come the physical sign such as a warm handshake, a hug, or whatever you feel comfortable with that seems appropriate. Any attempt to communicate acceptance and love can help the other person eventually reach a greater degree of self-acceptance and self-affirmation than was possible before the

Fifth Step. No self-acceptance is possible, Tillich reminds us, if we are not accepted in a person-to-person relationship. "A wall to which I confess cannot forgive me," he has written, and "acceptance by something which is less than personal could never overcome personal self-rejection." Under no circumstances is a minister to appear righteous, hard, or arrogant, for people who come to him "seek a love which is rooted in forgiveness, and this the righteous ones cannot give."[20]

This acceptance and forgiveness is directly related to the experience of inner healing which may be occurring throughout the Fifth Step: the healing of memories related to grief and loss, of wounds related to anger, resentments, pride; the transformation of guilt and self-hatred into compassion and gratitude. Such healing, however, cannot be equated with the minister's own talents, sensitivity, or personal charisma, since the experience of healing involves a reciprocal process—not dependent upon only one, but both participants. It is a power rooted in each person which, when shared, transforms both in some mysterious way. For the minister to identify himself fully as *the* healer in this process is an often subtle, sometimes blatant form of "savior complex" which can eventually drive him mad.[21] Recalling Jesus' own words to the sick woman who reached out to him for help, "*Your* faith restored you to health" (Mark 5:34), the minister can help healing by activating in the other person the power which he or she already holds. He should also know from his own experience as well as the ongoing wisdom of the church and A.A. that any power of healing ultimately lies with the Higher Power who is God. It is with this humble acknowledgment that effective ministry inside and outside the Fifth Step is founded.

With such humility and trust, the Fifth Step itself must end. After being a sign of reconciliation with words of acceptance and love, you should terminate Step Five by letting go of it, knowing that in having done the best you could, the rest is in God's hands. You also need to be aware that as you continue to minister in Fifth Steps and to encourage others to participate in them that you remind all people—whether they are chemically dependent or not—of the value of "speaking the truth to one another" since "we are all parts of one another"; how only with "unveiled faces" can we reflect "like mirrors the brightness of the Lord."[22] It is also your *human* presence of care which might eventually help them discern and discover, experience and name the *transcendent* "power greater" than themselves.

Conclusion

"Every man and woman has a story to tell," my great, great grandfather wrote many years ago while telling his own story about migrating from Ireland to Minnesota.[23] His wisdom is confirmed by A.A. Not only does every person have a story, but there is a need, A.A. says, to share it; to verbally acknowledge the things that divide us as well as the things for which we can and should give thanks. Ministry itself, we have learned, is dependent upon listening with compassion to others' stories and sharing our own. Through such events of mutual self-revelation, we often discover common roots and experience a healing of our pasts, the transformation of weakness into strength, despair into hope, isolation into community.

For Christians, stories and story-telling are not a new phenomenon. Our roots go back to the story of a story-teller, a man who because of the healing power and significance of His words became identified as "the Word, who is life" (I John 1:1). However, for many people that story and His stories are lacking in power and meaning because of over-familiarity. They fail to see that His story is *the* story of their lives, or to affirm the value of their stories as reflections of His. But when we share our stories and reflect together upon them, when we together seek to discern the traces of God's love, we begin to discover that our stories, like His, are full of laughter and tears, anguish and surrender, death and new life. We also begin to see that the new God of acceptance and forgiveness discovered in the stories we share is the same God of old, the God of our ancestors who "lives among men," who "makes His home among them," whose name is "God-with-them," who "wipes away all tears" (Revelation 21:1-4). It is then that a sense of wonder is born; that we are united with what the Jewish writer, Abraham Heschel, calls "the great yearning that sweeps eternity: the yearning to praise, the yearning to serve."[24]

Notes

[1] For a history and explanation of the Oxford Group Movement, see Walter Clark, *The Oxford Group: Its History and Significance* (New York: Bookman Associates, 1951), and Irving Benson, *The Eight Points of the Oxford Group* (London: Oxford University Press, 1936).

[2] Alcoholics Anonymous, *Alcoholics Anonymous Comes of Age* (New York: A.A. World Services, 1957), p. 44. For other sources regarding the influence of Christian churchmen upon A.A., see Leonard Blumberg, "The Ideology of a Therapeutic Social Movement: Alcoholics Anonymous," *Journal of Studies on Alcohol*, vol. 38, no. 11, 1977: 2134-2139, and Robert Thomsen, *Bill W.* (New York: Harper & Row, 1975), especially pp. 307-316.

[3] Alcoholics Anonymous, *Alcoholics Anonymous*, (New York: A.A. World Services, 1952) p. xv. It wasn't June, however, but Mother's Day when the two men met. See *Alcoholics Anonymous Comes of Age*, p. 67.

[4] This definition is found in most A.A. literature and brochures.

[5] For an explanation of Step Five, see especially *Alcoholics Anonymous,* pp. 72-75, and, Alcoholics Anonymous, *Twelve Steps and Twelve Traditions* (New York: A.A. World Services, 1952), pp. 56-63. The summary and quotations in this booklet are taken from those pages.

[6] Bill Wilson, *Three Talks to Medical Societies by Bill W.* (New York: A.A. World Services, n.d.), pp. 23-24.

[7] Alcoholics Anonymous, *Twelve Steps and Twelve Traditions,* p. 63.

[8] *Ibid.,* pp. 90-97.

[9] *Ibid.,* p. 63.

[10] Alcoholics Anonymous, *Alcoholics Anonymous,* p. 95.

[11] See, for example, the works of Sidney Jourard, especially his *Disclosing Man to Himself* (Princeton: D. Van Nostrand, 1968), and *The Transparent Self* (New York: D. Van Nostrand, 1971). Also my own doctoral dissertation, *The Event of Self-Revelation in the Reconciliation Process: A Pastoral Theological Comparison of A.A.'s Fifth Step and the Sacrament of Penance* (Ann Arbor, Mich.: Xerox Microfilms, 1981).

[12] For an examination of the value and history of the spiritual guide, see Kenneth Leech, *Soul Friend* (London: Sheldon Press, 1978), John T. McNeill, *A History of the Cure of Souls* (New York: Harper Torchbooks, 1965), Henri Nouwen, *The Way of the Heart* (New York: Seabury Press, 1981) and Tilden Edwards, *Spiritual Friend* (New York: Paulist Press, 1980). For a full discussion of the concept, "wounded healer," see Henri Nouwen, *The Wounded Healer* (Garden City, NY: Doubleday, 1972); also, his *Creative Ministry* (Garden City, NY: Doubleday, 1971).

[13] See Carl G. Jung, *Psychology and Religion: West and East* (Princeton: Princeton University Press, 1973), pp. 327-347.

[14] *Idem, Modern Man in Search of a Soul* (New York: A Harvest Book, 1933), p. 51.

[15] See the reflective exercises in James and Evelyn Whitehead, *Christian Life Patterns* (Garden City, NY: Doubleday, 1979). Other valuable sources that help one reflect on one's life story are Sam Keen, *To A Dancing God* (New York: Harper & Row, 1970), and Michael Novak, *Ascent of the Mountain, Flight of the Dove* (New York: Harper & Row, 1971).

[16] See Jung, *The Practice of Psychotherapy* (Princeton: Princeton University Press, 1966), pp. 8-9, and *Memories, Dreams, Reflections* (New York: Vintage Books, 1961), p. 133.

[17] Paul Tillich, *The New Being* (New York: Charles Scribner's Sons, 1955), p. 13, and *The Courage To Be* (New York: Charles Scribner's Sons, 1952), p. 165.

[18] *Idem, The Courage to Be,* pp. 165-167.

[19] For insight into the penitential process which culminated with a communal celebration and a sign of forgiveness, often the imposition of hands, see Jose Ramos-Regidor, "Reconciliation in the Primitive Church and its Lessons for Theology and Pastoral Practice Today," *Sacramental Reconciliation*, edited by Edward Schillebeeckx (New York: Seabury, 1971), pp. 76-88.

[20] See Tillich, *The Courage To Be*, pp. 165-167, and *The New Being*, pp. 3-14.

[21] See the excellent book by Adolf Guggenbuhl-Craig, *Power in the Helping Professions* (New York: Spring Publications, 1971), for an analysis of the healer archetype and the dangers of anyone totally identifying with it.

[22] James 5:16; Ephesians 4:25-26; II Corinthians 3:18.

[23] Martin Foy, "The Trials and Experience of Frontier Life on the Western Prairie," *The Story of Cormac*, edited by Father Hunt (Toronto, Ontario: Mission Press, 1954).

[24] Abraham Heschel, *Man is not Alone* (New York: Farrar, Straus, and Giroux, 1951), p. 259.